NBA ALL-TIME SUPER SCORERS

by James Buckley, Jr.

SCHOLASTIC INC.

New York　Toronto　London　Auckland　Sydney
Mexico City　New Delhi　Hong Kong　Buenos Aires

This book is for Siena, a slam dunk superstar!

PHOTO CREDITS
NBA Entertainment Photos
Cover (Jordan), 24, 34, 47 (Jordan): Nathaniel S. Butler.
Cover (O'Neal), 5, 15, 23, 32, 38, 47 (Bryant): Andrew D. Bernstein.
Cover (Iverson), 37: Jesse D. Garrabrant.
Cover (Chamberlain), 7, 10, 11, 12, 14, 19: NBA Photo Library.
9: NBA Hall of Fame. 16: Jon Soohoo. 18: Scott Cunningham. 20: Bill Baptist.
22, 33: Fernando Medina. 26: Noren Trotman. 28: Thearon Henderson.
29, 31: Don Grayston. 40: Lou Capozzola. 42: Tim Defrisco.
43: Scott Cunningham. 44: Rocky Widner. 46: Ken Regan.

ISBN 0-439-34306-2

12 11 10 9 8 7 6 5 4 3 2 1   1 2 3 4 5 6/0 1

0100-57860- MM

796.323 Printed in the U.S.A.

BUC   First Scholastic printing, December 2001

Book design by Louise Bova

Contents

CHAPTER ONE

It's Good!

For more than 100 years, the object of basketball has been simple: score points by putting the ball in the basket. When Dr. James Naismith showed his YMCA students how to play the game in 1891, rule number eight read: "A goal shall be made when the ball is thrown . . . into the basket."

Nail the shot, make the bucket, swish, jam, drain . . . it's good! Whatever you call it, without scoring, the game of basketball would be nothing more than a bunch of people dribbling around.

Today, teams often pour in more than 100 points a game. But it wasn't always that way. During the first few years, scoring totals were low. Teams held onto the ball for a long time to get the perfect shot. Finally, in 1954, the NBA created the 24-second shot clock. Teams had to take a shot and score (or at least hit the rim) within 24 seconds of getting the ball. This sped up the game, and scoring totals shot up.

A Set of Shots

Players can score in dozens of different ways. Each type of shot calls upon different skills. Here are the most popular shots:

LAYUP: A player dribbles in as close as he can,

and then bounces the ball off the backboard or drops the ball straight into the basket.

JUMP SHOT: A player jumps in the air and flicks the ball toward the basket with one hand from above his head. A jumper can be taken from just about any-where on the floor. If the shot is made from out-side of an arc painted on the court, it is worth three points.

HOOK SHOT: With one shoulder

David Robinson

facing the basket, a player (usually a taller one) raises his opposite arm high above his head. With one hand he arcs, or hooks, the ball toward the basket.

SLAM DUNK: 1) Take ball. 2) Fly. 3) Slam ball through hoop. Easy, right? Players slam with one

OUTSIDE THE ARC

On each end of every NBA court is a painted arc. In the corners, the arc is 22 feet from the basket. At the top of the key, it's 23 feet 9 inches away. Make a shot from behind that arc, and it's worth three points. The NBA introduced the three-point shot in 1979.

Teams soon began to realize the power of a shot worth three points. Offenses started to "kick the ball out" to a shooter waiting behind the arc. Sharpshooters who specialized in nailing the "trey" began to emerge.

Today, no NBA game is complete without a hailstorm of threes flying toward the basket. The all-time leader in three-point shots made is Reggie Miller of the Indiana Pacers, who has made more than 2,000.

hand, with two hands, overhand, from between their legs, after spinning in circles or any other way they can think of that gets a crowd roaring and opponents grumbling.

A Nose for the Basket

During the game, any player can score for his team. That is one of the beautiful things about basketball. Just about every player who plays gets at least a few cracks at the basket.

But while every player *can* score, every player doesn't.

Throughout NBA history, there have been players who seem to have a special nose for the basket. They might use their size to power to the hoop or tower over the opposition. They might use slashing speed to move around to find open shots. They might

George Mikan

just have perfect aim on their jump shots.

Whatever it is and however they do it, some guys just score — a lot. They rack up points faster than ice cream disappears after dinner.

This book is about those guys . . . the best scorers in NBA history.

Early Point Machines

The first professional player to make his mark as a scoring machine was George Mikan. At 6-10, he was one of the biggest players in the early years of the NBA. He was also one of the best. Shooting hook shots with either hand and two-handed set shots, Mikan led the NBL in scoring twice, the BAA once and the NBA three times while helping the Minneapolis Lakers win one BAA Championship along with four NBA titles.

Mikan was so good that Madison Square Garden once put up a sign that read simply: TONIGHT — GEO. MIKAN VS. KNICKS. His career average of 23.1 points per game is still among the all-time top 20, which is amazing considering all the great players who have followed him.

Another early super scorer was "Jumpin'" Joe Fulks. This master of the jump shot learned the tricks of his trade shooting tin cans through a hoop in his parents' barn in Kentucky. When he got his hands on a real ball, there was no stopping him. He was among the top scorers in every pro league he played in.

On February 10, 1949, Fulks did something that still is one of basketball's most amazing feats. In a time when teams scored only about 80 points a game, Fulks scored 63!

"They give me the ball and I shoot it," he said. "That's all there is to it."

As you read these stories of other NBA super scorers, you'll see there's a lot more to it than that!

Jumpin' Joe Fulks

CHAPTER TWO

The Big Dipper: Wilt Chamberlain

Would you believe it if someone told you that an NBA player once scored 100 points in a game? What if you were told that same player averaged more than 50 points a game . . . for an entire season? Or that he also averaged nearly 40 points a game throughout seven seasons?

Well, believe it or not, all those things are true, and they were all accomplished by one incredible player: Wilt Chamberlain.

The Dipper was one of the NBA's most dominant forces. He was the NBA scoring champion in each of his first seven seasons in the NBA (1959–1966). He was a classic center at 7-1, and he used an awesome variety of shots to reach his huge points totals.

Growing up in Philadelphia, Wilt scored as many as 70 points in a high school game three times, once scoring 60 points in only 12 minutes. He earned one of his many nicknames, "The Big Dipper," after he had to dip his head under some low pipes in his school because he was so tall. In college, he set a school record at Kansas with 53 points. He later led Kansas to the national title game.

Joining the NBA in 1959, Chamberlain was named both the NBA Rookie of the Year and MVP after leading the league with an average of 37.6 points per game. His greatest scoring season came in 1961–62, when he averaged an awesome 50.4 points per game and became the only player to score more than 4,000 points in a season.

STATS STUFF

How to figure points per game (ppg): Divide the total number of points a player scores in a season by the number of games he plays. Since 1969, the NBA scoring title has been awarded to the player with the highest ppg average.

Example: In 1961–62, Wilt Chamberlain scored 4,029 points and played in 80 games.

4,029/80 = 50.4

Wilt's scoring binge reached its height with his incredible 100-point performance on March 2, 1962. Early in the game, Wilt's Philadelphia Warriors teammates knew that the Dipper was hot and kept feeding him the ball. As the game went on, the shots continued to pour in from every angle. Chamberlain, who had never been a good free throw shooter, even made a career-best 28 of 32 free throw attempts.

In the end, Chamberlain scored his 100th point on a dunk with just 42 seconds remaining in the game. Fans swarmed the court to congratulate him on his amazing performance.

Not surprisingly, Chamberlain said afterward, "It was my greatest game."

Chamberlain continued his stunning scoring for the rest of the decade, moving with the Warriors to San Francisco and then returning to Philadelphia as the leader of the 76ers. He led the 76ers to the NBA title in 1967 and later helped the Lakers win the title in 1972. When Wilt retired, he was the NBA's all-time leading scorer and held most of the game's scoring records.

MIND-BOGGLING!

Here are some of the Big Dipper's other amazing scoring feats.

- In December 1961, he scored 40 or more points in 14 games in a row. He matched that streak in January and February of 1962.
- In December 1961, he set a single-game record with 78 points. But that record didn't stand for long! Wilt broke his own record four months later in March of 1962.
- He scored 50 or more points in 118 games and 40 or more points in 271 games.
- He has 15 of the NBA's top 20 single-game scoring performances.
- His 30.1 points per game career average is the second-highest of all time.

CHAPTER THREE

Kareem and the Sky-Hook

Kareem Abdul-Jabbar used his height and his soft touch to create one of the most unstoppable shots in NBA history—the sky-hook.

Using that shot (and many others), Kareem won six NBA MVP Awards, played in a record 18 All-Star Games, and became the NBA's all-time leader in total points.

After crushing opponents in New York high school basketball, the young man who was then known as Lew Alcindor (see box) helped UCLA win three NCAA championships. He joined the Milwaukee Bucks in 1969 and poured in 28.8 points per game to win the Rookie of the Year Award.

After earning one scoring title and helping Milwaukee win an NBA title, Abdul-Jabbar left the Bucks and joined the Los Angeles Lakers in 1975. In 1979, after Magic Johnson joined the team, the duo led the Lakers to five NBA titles during the 1980s. With Kareem scoring points, blocking shots and defending big men, and Magic running the offense, the Lakers were the best team of the decade.

Throughout his long career, Kareem kept himself in excellent shape and was very agile for someone so tall (7-2). His greatest weapon was the mighty sky-hook, which he developed in high school and college against much smaller opponents. But it worked perfectly in the pros, too. In the sky-hook, Kareem used one of his long arms to stretch the ball way over his head. When he rose up on one leg and jumped slightly, the ball was often over the level of the basket. With a flick of his wrist, the ball left his hand and zipped on a low arc toward the basket. From anywhere inside 18 feet or so, the shot was deadly . . . and impossible to stop.

Kareem's scoring feats are stunning: He scored 10 or

more points in 787 straight games. He scored nearly 5,000 points more than the second all-time leading scorer, Karl Malone. He averaged 20 points per game or more every season from 1969–1986. In 1984, he scored his 31,420th point to overtake Wilt Chamberlain and become the all-time leading scorer in NBA history. "The Big Fella" was at the top of the charts, and he remains there today with an incredible 38,387 career points.

CLUTCH WHEN IT COUNTED

When he retired, Abdul-Jabbar was the NBA's all-time playoff scoring leader. He helped his teams win six NBA championships and earn 18 playoff appearances. In the postseason, Kareem was Mr. Clutch. Here are some of his greatest NBA Finals scoring feats.

- 1971: Named NBA Finals MVP. Averaged 27 points per game while leading the Bucks to the second Finals sweep in NBA history.

- 1980: Scored 33, 38, 33 and 40 points before injuring his ankle. The Lakers won the series in six games.

- 1985: At age 38, Kareem was again named Finals MVP. Scored 36 points in Game 5, 29 points in title-clinching Game 6, and averaged 30.2 points in the series.

- After playing a record 237 postseason games, Kareem retired as the NBA's all-time leading playoff scorer with 5,762 points. (Michael Jordan later topped that total.)

CHAPTER FOUR

The Iceman: George Gervin

Few NBA players have scored as many points with as much flair as George Gervin, who was known as "The Iceman." Gervin was a gifted outside shooter who also could drive to the hoop to use his patented finger roll shot. Only three other players have scored in double figures in as many straight games as Gervin, who reached at least 10 points in 407 games in a row.

Gervin was almost cut from his high school team. He had to get extra practice with the school janitor late at night. But once he grew, his game improved. After playing at Eastern Michigan University, Gervin began his pro career in 1972 in the American Basketball Association (ABA).

The ABA was formed in 1967 as a rival to the NBA. Using a red-white-and-blue-striped ball and a wide-open style of play, the ABA delighted fans. Gervin played his first two seasons with the Virginia Squires. When he joined the San Antonio Spurs in 1974, his points really started adding up. From 1974 to 1976, Gervin was among the ABA's top scorers. His smooth-as-glass style was paying off, and he could hit just about any shot from just about any angle.

Several ABA teams, including the Spurs, joined the NBA for the 1976–77 season. Gervin's NBA opponents soon learned about the slick-shooting Iceman. He was the NBA's leading scorer in 1978, 1979, 1980 and 1982. Only Michael Jordan and Wilt Chamberlain have won more scoring titles.

Gervin made his points quietly, without the flash and dash of other

players in those years. But players knew about his awesome gifts. "He's the only guy I'd pay to see play," NBA great Jerry West once said.

"You don't stop George Gervin," said opposing coach Dick Motta. "You just hope his arm gets tired after forty shots. The guy can score anytime he wants to."

George wanted to score often enough to pile up a career average of 26.2 ppg, the seventh highest in NBA history.

DOWN TO THE LAST GAME

Gervin was the winner of the closest scoring race in NBA history. On the final day of the 1977–78 season, David Thompson of Denver scored an amazing 73 points to finish the season with a 27.15 ppg average. The Iceman knew that he had to score 58 points that night to claim his first NBA scoring crown.

His teammates helped out, feeding him the basketball every time he was near the basket. But he missed his first five shots. Those 58 points seemed far away. Soon he cleared away the butterflies and got 20 points in the first quarter and an NBA-record 33 in the second. Just after the half, George got his 58th point. In only 33 minutes, the Iceman had done what he had to do to win the title. He finished the game with a franchise-record and career-best 63 points.

FINAL SCORING AVERAGES:
Gervin: 27.22
Thompson: 27.15

CHAPTER FIVE

When it comes to scoring, the name Michael Jordan stands out.

Jordan ignored the laws of physics, opponents and even pain to score and score and score. He scored on layups, on soft-touch jumpers, from long range, from the line and, of course, via his gravity-defying, crowd-thrilling, opponent-destroying slams.

From 1986 to 1993, Jordan matched Wilt Chamberlain by winning seven consecutive scoring titles. "MJ" was also perhaps the greatest clutch shooter in history. When the game, the playoff series or the season was on the line, Jordan wanted to take the shot . . . and he usually made it.

Jordan joined the Chicago Bulls in 1984, two years after making the basket that won the NCAA Championship for the University of North Carolina. The summer before he joined the Bulls, however, he earned a chance to help the United States win a

gold medal at the Summer Olympics in Los Angeles. His early NBA games were golden, too. Jordan scored 37 points in his third pro game. He had 45 in his eighth game, plus 25 or more in 10 of his first 15 games. Of course, he went on to win the Rookie of the Year Award. His mantel would soon be crowded with more metal than a hardware store.

Michael was still just warming up. He scored a playoff-record 63 points in 1986. In 1987, he won the first of his seven scoring titles. His 37.1 ppg average that year was the best in NBA history for a player under 7 feet tall. Though he was racking up some huge points totals, Michael was missing the one thing that he truly wanted: an NBA championship.

BIG FIVE

Here are Michael Jordan's top five highest single-game point totals.

1. 69 at Cleveland, March 28, 1990
2. 64 vs. Orlando, January 16, 1993
3. 63 at Boston, April 20, 1986 (playoffs)
4. 61 at Detroit, March 4, 1987
5. 61 vs. Atlanta, April 16, 1987

He didn't have to wait much longer. Joined by Scottie Pippen, Horace Grant and others, Jordan led the Bulls to the top of the mountain each year from 1991 to 1993. Michael averaged an amazing 41 ppg in the 1993 NBA Finals! Chicago was only the third franchise to win three straight titles.

But then, one of the greatest scoring machines of all time retired . . . to play baseball! His fans were stunned. But Michael missed the court, and soon he was back. It was as if he had never left.

In 1995–96, his first full season back, Michael won the first of three more scoring titles. He would end up with an all-time-best 10 scoring championships, tying Wilt's mark. He was also the NBA Finals MVP again. In 1997–98, he and the Bulls wrapped up another incredible three-peat. Jordan averaged 33.5 points in the NBA Finals to earn his sixth Finals MVP trophy.

As great as Michael was in the regular season, it was in the playoffs that he ruled. He scored 50 or more points in eight different playoff games. In 1992, he averaged more than 34 points in the team's 22 playoff games. In 1997, he scored fewer than 27 points in only three of the Bulls' 19 playoff games. When the title was at stake, Michael raised the level of his amazing game even higher.

He was fabulous in All-Star Games, too. He played in 11 of them, and won the MVP award three times. In 1997, Michael became the first player to record a triple-double in that game, with 14 points, 11 rebounds and 11 assists. His career average of 21.3 points in All-Star Games is also an all-time best.

You could fill an encyclopedia with Michael's records or a DVD with clips of his highlight shots. Jordan definitely had the touch. He had a feel for the basket

GAME WINNERS

Here is a sampling of MJ's greatest game-winning baskets in the NBA Playoffs.

1. **4/24/85:** A jumper from the corner forces Game 4 in a 1985 playoff series against Milwaukee in MJ's rookie season.

2. **5/7/89:** "The Shot," a jumper that won the Bulls' first-round playoff series against Cleveland. Jordan seems to hang in the air forever before taking the shot.

3. **5/17/93:** "The Shot II," another game-winner against Cleveland, this time in the Eastern Conference Semifinals, which the Bulls swept, 4–0.

4. **6/11/97:** Though sick with the stomach flu, he scores 38 points, including a three-point basket that defeats Utah in Game 5 of the NBA Finals.

5. **6/14/98:** 17-foot jumper with 5.2 seconds left clinches the Bulls' sixth NBA title in Michael's final NBA game.

and a need to score that separates scoring machines from everyday players.

"You don't know how or when or what he's going to do," said ace defender Michael Cooper about guarding Jordan. "But you just know he's going to get that shot off."

And with Jordan, more than likely, that shot would go in and his team would dance off the court with another NBA championship trophy.

CHAPTER SIX

The Mailman: Karl Malone

Few NBA players can score with as much consistency as Karl Malone. A dominant inside force, the 6-9, 256-pound Malone helped the Utah Jazz post one of the NBA's best records in the 1990s. The Jazz knew that "The Mailman" would always deliver.

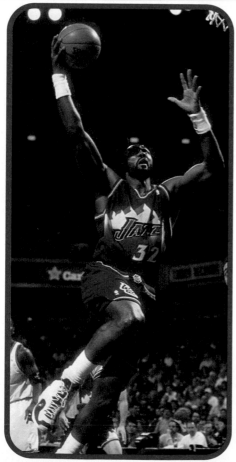

Malone used his power game to reach the number-two all-time spot on the NBA's scoring charts, with 32,919 points through the 2000–01 season. His scoring average of 25.9 points per game is eighth highest of all time.

Malone joined the Jazz as their first-round pick in 1986 out of Louisiana Tech. The Mailman quickly started making regular deliveries to the baskets of the NBA. Using a powerful game that combined post-up moves and perimeter jumpers, he averaged 25 ppg or more for 11 seasons, beginning in 1988.

Beginning in 1989, Malone was named to the All-NBA First Team for 10 straight seasons. He also began a string of six top-five finishes in the scoring race, including finishing second three times to Michael Jordan.

In 1996–97, the Mailman was named the NBA MVP after finishing second in scoring and helping lead the Jazz to the NBA Finals. The Mailman also led the Jazz to back-to-back NBA Finals appearances in 1997 and 1998 against the Chicago Bulls. In 1998–99, he won his second MVP trophy after finishing third in scoring. But the NBA championship has always escaped him.

Along with filling the basket from the paint, the Mailman also delivers from the free throw line. Many big men are not great free throw shooters. Wilt Chamberlain, for instance, was not a very good free throw shooter, though he was often fouled. Throughout his career, Malone has taken advantage of his many trips to the line. He regularly draws fouls from opponents who can't find any other way to stop his drives to the basket. Malone has made more free throws than any player in NBA history: 8,636.

Whether he's driving hard to the basket, lofting soft jumpers over outstretched defenders or dropping in free throw after free throw, the Mailman is a first-class scoring force.

A LITTLE HELP FROM HIS FRIEND

As great as Karl Malone and other NBA super scorers are, they can't play the game alone. Every good shooter needs teammates to give them good passes.

Malone and teammate John Stockton are the perfect example of how great scorers need a little help from their friends. Stockton, the Jazz point guard, is the NBA's all-time leader in assists with more than 14,000.

For 15 seasons, the two Utah Jazz stars have worked together to score and win. Malone has racked up the second-most points in NBA history, but he probably wouldn't have done it without Stockton.

John Stockton

Karl Malone

CHAPTER SEVEN

Shaq Daddy

He's quiet, sort of shy and great with kids. But on the basketball court . . . get out of his way! At 7-1 and more than 300 pounds, Shaquille O'Neal combines power and accuracy to make his shots like those of few players in history.

Twice a scoring champion, Shaq is always among league leaders in scoring (including finishing second three times). He also regularly

posts high field goal accuracy marks.

Shaq has been a star from his first NBA game, when he grabbed 18 rebounds. He quickly became a tough inside force for the Orlando Magic. He was the NBA Rookie of the Year for the 1992–93 season. He nearly won the scoring title the next year, but lost to David Robinson on the final day of the season.

In 1994–95, young Shaq took the Magic all the way to the NBA Finals. He moved to the Los Angeles Lakers for the 1996–97 season, but Shaq continued his high-scoring ways, averaging 26.2 points. In fact, "Shaq Daddy" has never averaged less than 26 points in a season since his rookie year. His great string of high scoring averages has helped him reach number three on the NBA's all-time points-per-game scoring list, behind only Michael Jordan and Wilt Chamberlain.

For all of Shaq's monster slams, hit rap albums and movie and TV appearances, his finest hours came at the end of the 1999–2000

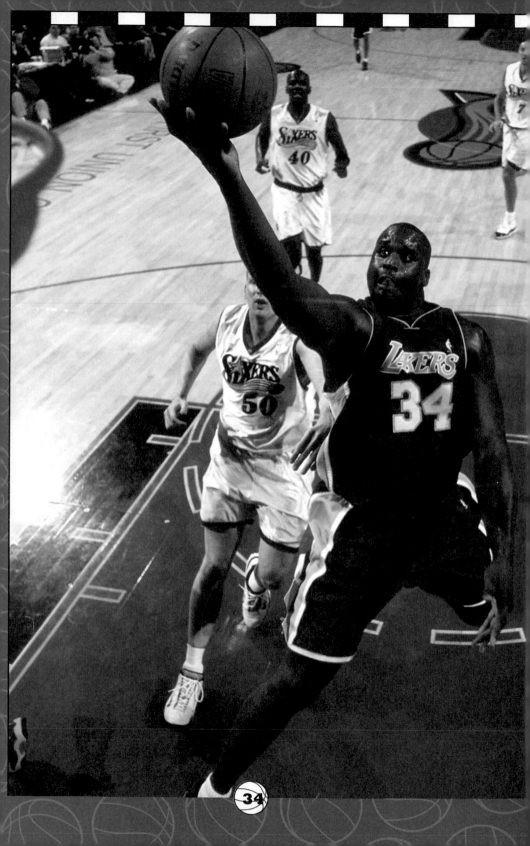

34

season. First, Shaq led the Lakers to the NBA's best record and won his second scoring title with a 29.7 ppg average. Then, he ruled in the playoffs. In the NBA Finals against Indiana, he averaged 38 points per game! The Lakers won their first title with Shaq at center, and he was named Finals MVP to go along with his season MVP Award.

In 2000–01, Shaq was third in scoring, with a 28.7 ppg average. He and Kobe Bryant led the Lakers on a record 15–1 playoff run that earned the Lakers their second straight NBA title. Those championships were dreams come true for the player that young fans think of as a big kid . . . a big kid who throws down the most tremendous dunks in the NBA!

SCORING TITLE DOESN'T ALWAYS EQUAL NBA TITLE

Having the top scorer in the NBA on your team doesn't mean you'll take home the NBA championship trophy. Many people have won scoring titles but not NBA titles: George Gervin with the Spurs; Bob McAdoo, a three-time scoring champion with Buffalo; "Pistol" Pete Maravich with New Orleans; and Shaq himself with Orlando. In fact, since the 1969–70 season, only three players have enjoyed that rare double play.

1970–71: Kareem Abdul-Jabbar, Bucks
1991–93: Michael Jordan, Bulls (3 titles)
1996–98: Michael Jordan, Bulls (3 titles)
1999–2000: Shaquille O'Neal, Lakers

CHAPTER EIGHT

Young Point Machines

With the exception of a few players, all the super scorers in this book have been big men. Whether that means the untouchable height of Mikan, Abdul-Jabbar and Chamberlain or the overall bulk of Malone and O'Neal, size has usually equaled major points.

In today's fast-paced game, however, dominant centers are more rare. And when they do play a big role on a team, they sometimes aren't the high scorers.

Many of the top young scorers in the NBA today are what some coaches call "slashers." They are skilled with the ball, run and move very fast and mix great jump-shooting ability with the skills to drive to the hoop. Today's best scorers are more like Gervin, and can shoot and score from anywhere at anytime. Plus, most of today's super scorers grew up playing a high school and college game that included the three-point shot. Mastering this long-range blast adds to their scoring totals.

While some big men — like Shaq and Tim Duncan — are still big scorers from a center or power forward position, most teams depend on players at other positions to score more. In 2000–01, Shaq was the only player in the top 10 in scoring who stood taller than 6-10.

Today's super scorers aren't small, of course, compared to the rest of the world. But among the tall trees of the NBA, more and more young saplings are rising to the top of the scoring charts.

Philadelphia's Allen Iverson is a perfect example. Though Iverson is just six feet tall, he is already a two-time scoring champion, including a league-best 31.1 average in 2000–01. He is able to use quickness and speed to rack up incredible point totals. Like Gervin, Iverson has mastered every type of shot and has no fear of shooting any time he has the ball, no matter who is guarding him. Iverson came into the league with his scoring touch. He wrapped up the 1996–97 Rookie of the Year

Allen Iverson

Kobe Bryant

Award with five straight 40-point games, scoring 50 points in the final game to seal the deal. Two years later, he led the league with a 26.8 ppg average. And he had seven 40-point games the following season before returning to the top of the scoring charts in 2001. The 2000–01 MVP put on quite a show during the Eastern Conference Semifinals by scoring 50-plus points twice! In the NBA Finals, he averaged 35.6 ppg against the Lakers.

Lakers guard Kobe Bryant is another of today's super scorers. Kobe stands 6-7, well below Shaq's 7-1. But Kobe combines a deadly outside shot with great leaping ability to make size less important. Bryant helped Shaq lead the Lakers to back-to-back NBA titles. Kobe is a fan favorite because of his huge number of high-flying moves and his long-distance shooting. In 2000–01, he teamed with Shaq to give the Lakers the best one-two scoring punch in the league: Shaq finished third and Kobe fourth in scoring. In the playoffs, Kobe had five games with 30 or more points.

Bryant's greatest skills are around the basket, but defenders can't give him room outside or he'll score every time. Not only does he create high-light-reel jams, he is a 30 percent shooter from three-point land.

Another young high scorer is Tracy McGrady of the Orlando Magic. McGrady looks thin, but his 6-8 frame hides the heart of a scoring machine. Like Kobe, McGrady is equally comfortable shooting from outside or heading for the net. In 2000–01, he had a breakout season, finishing seventh in the league with a 26.8 ppg average, and leading all NBA playoff scorers with a 33.8 ppg average. He set a career high with 49 points in an April game. Orlando fans are looking for more T-Mac Magic in the future.

Jerry Stackhouse played college ball at North Carolina, the same school as Michael Jordan. Perhaps Jordan left some tips behind at

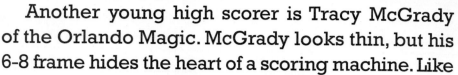

Tracy McGrady

his old school, because Stackhouse has become one of the league's hottest young scorers. A 29.8 ppg average placed the Detroit Pistons' forward second behind Iverson in the scoring race in 2000–01.

MILLENNIUM MADNESS

The new century dawned with basketballs pouring into NBA nets. Here are the best single-game scoring performances from the 2000–01 season. See anyone familiar?

57 JERRY STACKHOUSE, Detroit at Chicago, April 3, 2001

54 ALLEN IVERSON, Philadelphia at Cleveland, January 6, 2001

53 TONY DELK, Phoenix at Sacramento, January 2, 2001 (OT)

51 ANTAWN JAMISON, Golden State at Seattle, December 3, 2000

51 ANTAWN JAMISON, Golden State vs. L.A. Lakers, December 6, 2000 (OT)

51 KOBE BRYANT, L.A. Lakers at Golden State, December 6, 2000 (OT)

51 CHRIS WEBBER, Sacramento vs. Indiana, January 5, 2001 (OT)

51 ALLEN IVERSON, Philadelphia vs. Toronto, January 21, 2001 (OT)

(OT = overtime game)

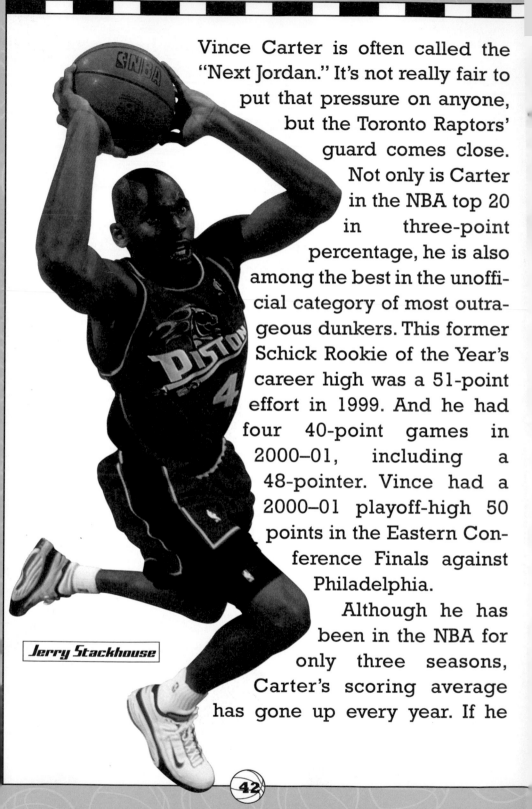

Vince Carter is often called the "Next Jordan." It's not really fair to put that pressure on anyone, but the Toronto Raptors' guard comes close. Not only is Carter in the NBA top 20 in three-point percentage, he is also among the best in the unofficial category of most outrageous dunkers. This former Schick Rookie of the Year's career high was a 51-point effort in 1999. And he had four 40-point games in 2000–01, including a 48-pointer. Vince had a 2000–01 playoff-high 50 points in the Eastern Conference Finals against Philadelphia.

Although he has been in the NBA for only three seasons, Carter's scoring average has gone up every year. If he

Jerry Stackhouse

Vince Carter

Antawn Jamison

can continue that, he might be battling Shaq, Iverson and Stackhouse for scoring honors for many years to come.

Our final young super scorer is another North Carolina product. Golden State Warriors forward Antawn Jamison jumped into the ranks of the super scorers by opening 2000–01 with five

GETTIN' OFF ON THE RIGHT FOOT

Each season, hot young players join the NBA, hoping to join the ranks of the super scorers featured in this book. Some of them get off to fast starts. Here are some of the best performances by players in their first pro seasons.

Most points by a rookie in a single game

58	Wilt Chamberlain, Philadelphia vs. Detroit, January 25, 1960
58	Wilt Chamberlain, Philadelphia at New York, February 21, 1960
57	Rick Barry, San Francisco at New York, December 14, 1965
56	Earl Monroe, Baltimore vs. Los Angeles, February 13, 1968 (OT)

Highest ppg average for a rookie season

37.6	Wilt Chamberlain, Philadelphia, 1959–60
31.6	Walt Bellamy, Chicago, 1961–62
30.5	Oscar Robertson, Cincinnati, 1960–61

Each February, the NBA gathers its brightest lights (and, not surprisingly, most of its top scorers) for the annual NBA All-Star Game. Here are some noteworthy All-Star Game scoring performances.

- Most points, career: Kareem Abdul-Jabbar, 251 (18 games)
- Most points, game: Wilt Chamberlain, 42 (1962)
- Highest career ppg average (minimum total points: 60 points): Michael Jordan, 21.3*

* Allen Iverson has averaged 25.5 points in his two All-Star Games. But he has a total of only 51 points. At that rate, he'll only need one more game to take this record from MJ.

straight games of 30 or more points. In December of that year, he really busted out, putting up back-to-back 51-point games. Jamison ended the season ninth in the NBA, with a 24.9 ppg average.

Wilt Chamberlain

From Mikan to Wilt . . . from Abdul-Jabbar to MJ . . . from big stars of today like Shaq and the Mailman to young slashers like Kobe and Iverson — as long as there has been basketball, there have been super scorers. Will you be the next one?

Michael Jordan

Kobe Bryant

Top-10 single-season scoring performances

Player, season	Points per game
1. Wilt Chamberlain, 1961–62	50.4
2. Wilt Chamberlain, 1962–63	44.8
3. Wilt Chamberlain, 1960–61	38.4
4. Wilt Chamberlain, 1959–60	37.6
5. Michael Jordan, 1986–87	37.1
6. Michael Jordan, 1987–88	35.0
7. Kareem Abdul-Jabbar, 1971–72	34.8
8. Rick Barry, 1966–67	34.7
9. Bob McAdoo, 1974–75	34.5
10. Nate Archibald, 1972–73	34.0

Top-10 career scoring leaders; total points (through 2000–2001 season)

Player	Total points
1. Kareem Abdul-Jabbar	38,387
2. Karl Malone*	32,919
3. Wilt Chamberlain	31,419
4. Michael Jordan	29,277
5. Moses Malone	27,409
6. Elvin Hayes	27,313
7. Oscar Robertson	26,710
8. Dominique Wilkins	26,688
9. Hakeem Olajuwon*	26,511
10. John Havlicek	26,395

* still playing